The Voice of the Martyrs

PO Box 443,
Bartlesville, OK 74005

The Story of
St. Nicholas
MORE THAN REINDEER AND A RED SUIT

Cheryl Odden

*Illustrated by R.F. Palavicini
and Castle Animation*

The Voice of the Martyrs is a nonprofit, Christian organization dedicated to helping Christians who are persecuted for their faith in communist, Islamic and other nations hostile to Christ. In 1967, Richard and Sabina Wurmbrand started the ministry of VOM. Having been imprisoned in communist Romania for their work with the underground church, their vision soon became global, and a network of offices was birthed to raise awareness of today's courageous persecuted church and take relief to those who suffer for their Christian witness.

For a free, monthly newsletter and ways you can help today's persecuted church, contact:

The Voice of the Martyrs
PO Box 443
Bartlesville, OK 74005
(800) 747-0085
E-mail: thevoice@vom-usa.org
Website: www.persecution.com

For Ainsley and Chaney.
May the generous and tenacious faith of Nicholas
inspire you to stand for Jesus…
no matter what!
Love, Mom

For our persecuted brethren,
who, like Nicholas,
dare to stand up for Jesus,
risking imprisonment and death.

A Note from the Author to Parents and Educators

Throughout history many legends about the life of Saint Nicholas of Myra have circulated around the world, bringing us to whom we know today as Santa Claus—a chubby man in a red suit who delivers presents to good boys and girls with his reindeer on Christmas Eve. But who is this man behind the myth of Santa Claus?

Nicholas of Myra was born in the third century in a province called Lycia, which was a part of the Roman Empire. Today ancient Lycia is a part of the country we know as Turkey. Nicholas is believed to have died around 343 A.D., on December 6th, a date that is currently celebrated by many nations, such as Germany, Switzerland and the Netherlands, where it is called "Saint Nicholas Day." For example, in Germany, children are known to put a boot, called a *Nikolaus-Stiefel*, outside their front door on the eve of Saint Nicholas Day, hoping he will fill it with gifts if he thinks they were good. But if found bad, they will receive a lump of charcoal.

The real Nicholas was a man full of generosity and conviction. He was born to wealthy parents who, when they died, left him their fortune. He chose to use his inheritance to help those in need. For example, one of the vignettes in the book is about three sisters who were saved from life on the streets. Their father was unable to arrange suitable marriages because he did not have enough money for their dowries. (Therefore, the father was left with no choice but to sell them to a brothel.) Upon hearing this, Nicholas secretly threw bags of gold into the girls' room. The father was elated and, after discovering his daughters' mysterious benefactor, was sworn to secrecy by Nicholas that he would never tell anyone who had given him the gold.

Nicholas is recorded to have exposed the corruptness of a government official during a famine. He uncovered the governor's deceitful actions of hoarding grain until the demand forced it into higher prices. Later, Nicholas intervened in an execution of three innocent men…all falsely accused by the same, crooked governor. It is said that one of the prisoners was situated on the block for decapitation, and Nicholas grabbed the sword from the executioner's hands, setting all three men free. He was praised for his bravery.

Even though many have preserved the stories of Nicholas' acts of righteousness, few know of his sufferings for Christ. When the Roman emperor Diocletian took power, he instigated a horrific persecution of Christians. Nicholas was imprisoned and physically tortured (pinched with hot iron pliers) for refusing to deny Jesus as God. One account mentions the prisons were so full of church leaders there was no room for the actual criminals.

After the reign of persecution ended, Nicholas would still face a fierce testing of his faith - this time within the church. A preacher named Arius began promoting a heresy that Jesus was not God in the flesh. Arius even went so far as to set his false teaching to music by putting words to popular drinking songs. Constantine, the new leader of the Roman Empire, called together church leaders at Nicea to discuss Arius' teachings and other issues dividing the church. This was called the Council of Nicea. According to legend, as Arius was making his presentation, he began singing one of his blasphemous songs about Jesus. Unwilling to see this man shame Christ, Nicholas stood up and punched Arius in the mouth. Those in attendance were shocked! Although they understood Nicholas' need to stand up for Christ's reputation, they did not believe they could allow such behavior since Christ taught us to love our enemies and live a life of peace. Therefore, Nicholas was no longer allowed to serve as bishop. (It's noted he was later restored to his position.) But this action did not stop Nicholas from serving the sick and needy.

The persecution of Christians is not confined to Nicholas' time in history. Those who choose to do what's right and follow God have been persecuted since the beginning of time. Even today Christians are being persecuted in communist and Islamic nations for knowing Jesus Christ and telling others about Him. In communist countries meeting for a Bible study in a home is considered illegal and owning a Bible could cause a person to be sentenced to several years in prison. In Islamic nations Muslims who convert to Christianity have been rejected by family members and even gunned down on the street by fanatical Muslims.

Those who are persecuted for following Christ today are much like Nicholas of Myra: They humbly serve their fellow countrymen and courageously stand for the Lord when faced with the choice of prison *with* Christ or no prison *without* Christ. His story of boldness and generosity in the face of persecution from the government and conflict within the church is for everyone. By any Christian definition, Nicholas was indeed a saint.

May Nicholas of Myra's life challenge us to live generously by serving the poor and courageously by standing for Christ in a culture that is increasingly hostile to Him and His people!

"Let's name him Nicholas."

A long time ago, about 200 years after the birth of Jesus, a little boy was born to wealthy parents in a land called Lycia.

"Let's name him Nicholas," they agreed and loved him with all their hearts.

But when Nicholas was still very young, his parents died and left him all of their money.

"I will use this to help the poor," Nicholas decided and so began his life of giving to those in need.

"I will use this to help the poor."

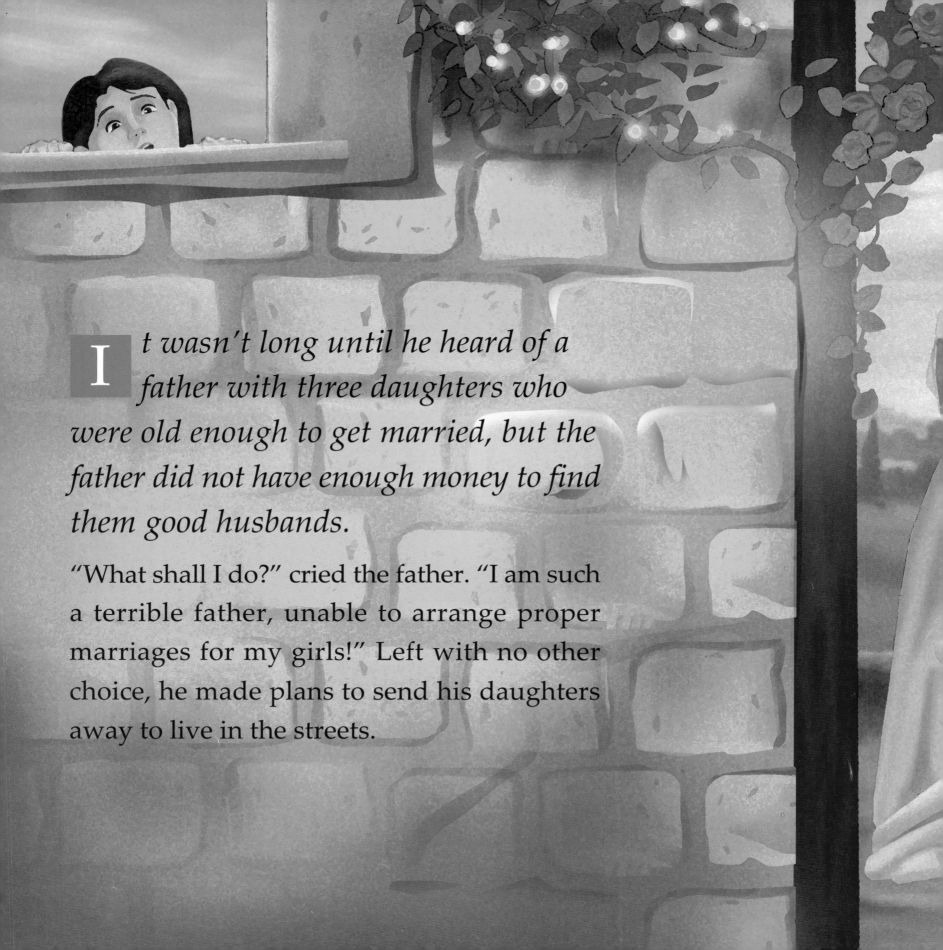

I t wasn't long until he heard of a father with three daughters who were old enough to get married, but the father did not have enough money to find them good husbands.

"What shall I do?" cried the father. "I am such a terrible father, unable to arrange proper marriages for my girls!" Left with no other choice, he made plans to send his daughters away to live in the streets.

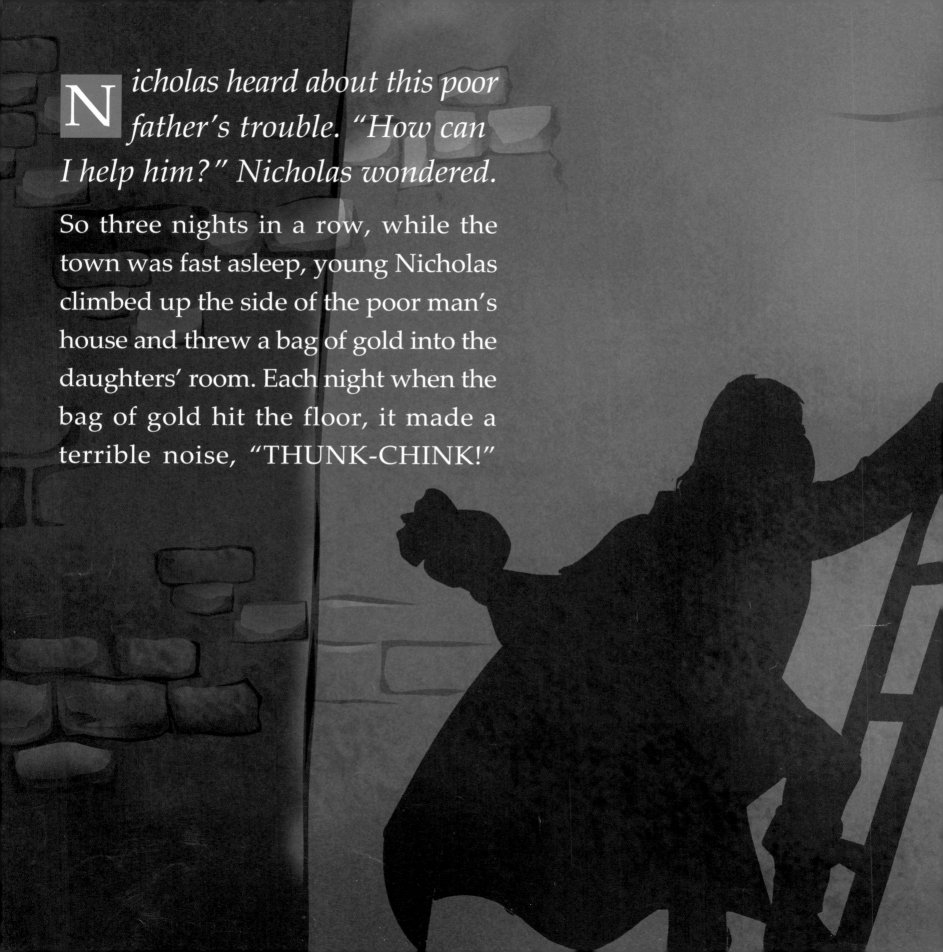

Nicholas heard about this poor father's trouble. "How can I help him?" Nicholas wondered.

So three nights in a row, while the town was fast asleep, young Nicholas climbed up the side of the poor man's house and threw a bag of gold into the daughters' room. Each night when the bag of gold hit the floor, it made a terrible noise, "THUNK-CHINK!"

Nicholas said,
"You cannot tell
anyone what I have
done for you!"

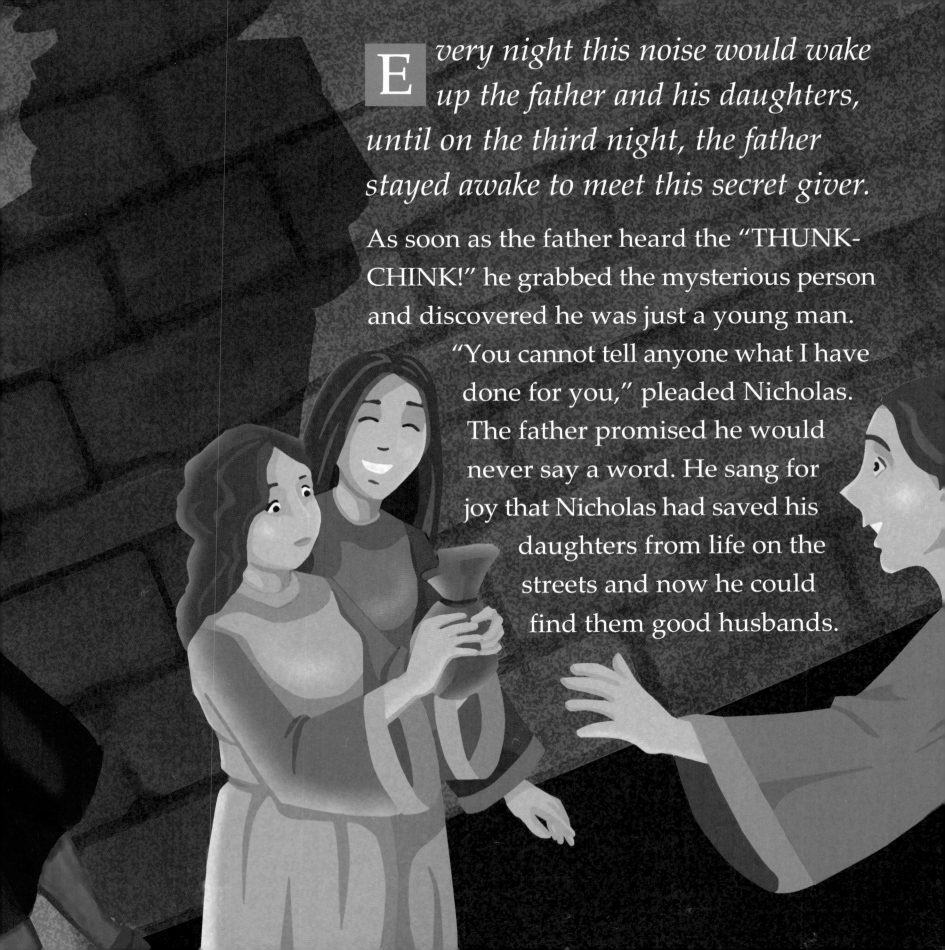

very night this noise would wake up the father and his daughters, until on the third night, the father stayed awake to meet this secret giver.

As soon as the father heard the "THUNK-CHINK!" he grabbed the mysterious person and discovered he was just a young man. "You cannot tell anyone what I have done for you," pleaded Nicholas. The father promised he would never say a word. He sang for joy that Nicholas had saved his daughters from life on the streets and now he could find them good husbands.

E ver since Nicholas was a boy,
he had a love for God's Word.

So one day, he decided to make a trip
to the Holy Land and visit the places he
had read about. He visited Bethlehem,
where Jesus was born, and even prayed
in the empty tomb where He rose from
the dead. "Jesus was truly Emmanuel,
God with us. My life will never be the
same!" Nicholas declared.

"My life will never be the same!"

S oon it was time for Nicholas to leave and return to his homeland. He boarded the ship, and he and the crew began the long voyage to Lycia. One night the winds began to blow and the waves began to rage, rousing Nicholas from his deep sleep.

"I don't think we're going to make it to shore safely!" warned the captain. So Nicholas bowed on the deck of the ship, and as his body was thrown back and forth, he prayed, "Dear Jesus, please lead us to shore safely, and I promise I will give thanks to You upon our arrival on land." The waters calmed, and again the ship carried on her steady course for a city called Myra. "Your prayers saved us!" cheered the crew.

"Dear Jesus, please lead us
to shore safely, and I promise
I will give thanks to You upon
our arrival on land."

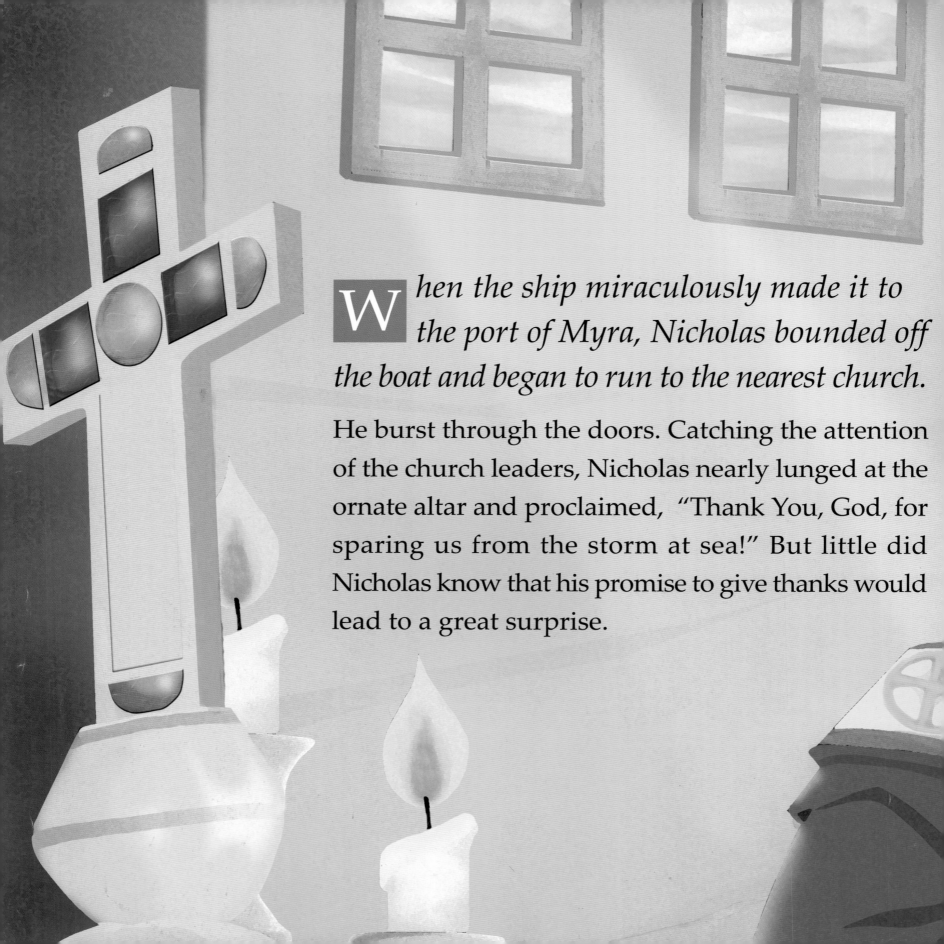

*W*hen the ship miraculously made it to the port of Myra, Nicholas bounded off the boat and began to run to the nearest church.

He burst through the doors. Catching the attention of the church leaders, Nicholas nearly lunged at the ornate altar and proclaimed, "Thank You, God, for sparing us from the storm at sea!" But little did Nicholas know that his promise to give thanks would lead to a great surprise.

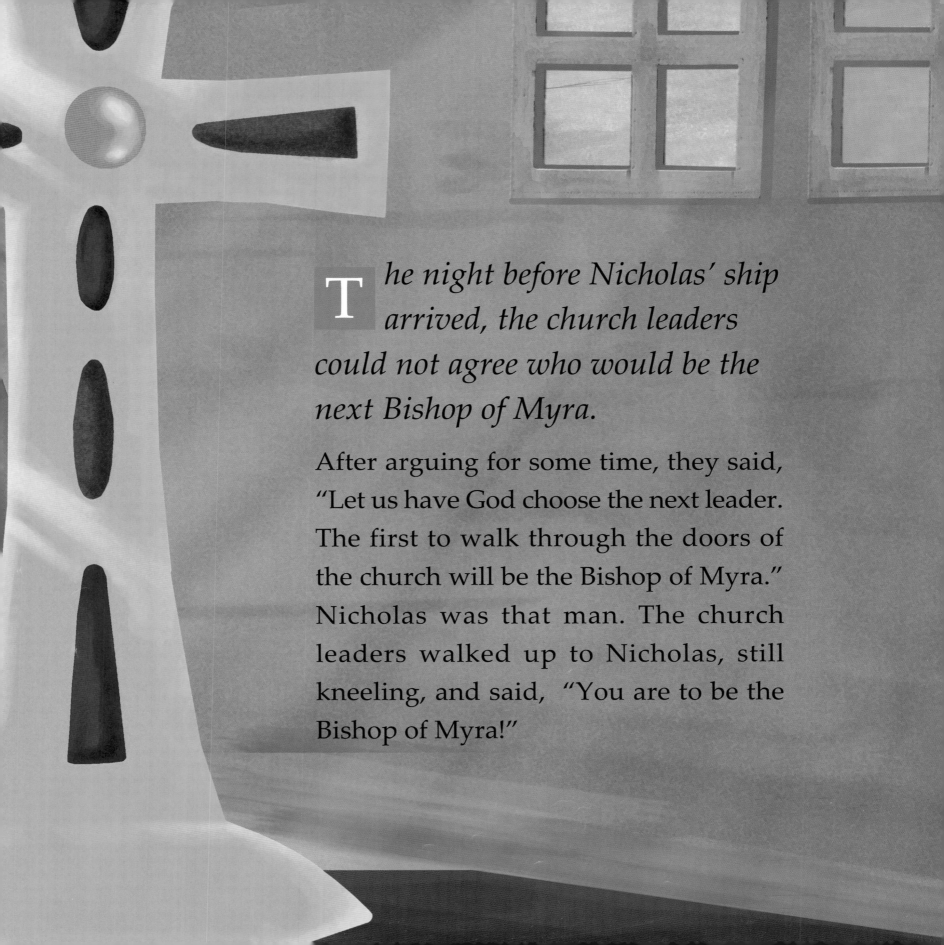

T*he night before Nicholas' ship arrived, the church leaders could not agree who would be the next Bishop of Myra.*

After arguing for some time, they said, "Let us have God choose the next leader. The first to walk through the doors of the church will be the Bishop of Myra." Nicholas was that man. The church leaders walked up to Nicholas, still kneeling, and said, "You are to be the Bishop of Myra!"

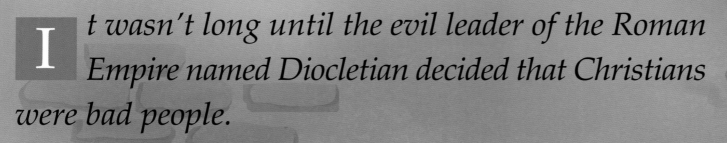

I t wasn't long until the evil leader of the Roman Empire named Diocletian decided that Christians were bad people.

Soon it was declared that it was a crime for people to own God's Word or any other book about God and His Son Jesus. "To the fire!" the officials demanded when God's Word was found in people's homes. And many Christians sadly watched the Word of Life burn to ashes. Some Christians were even sent to prison.

"To the fire!"

Despite the threat of imprisonment, Nicholas continued helping others in need.

But his love for Jesus was soon noticed by Roman officials. "Off to jail!" they said, and Nicholas was arrested and thrown into prison.

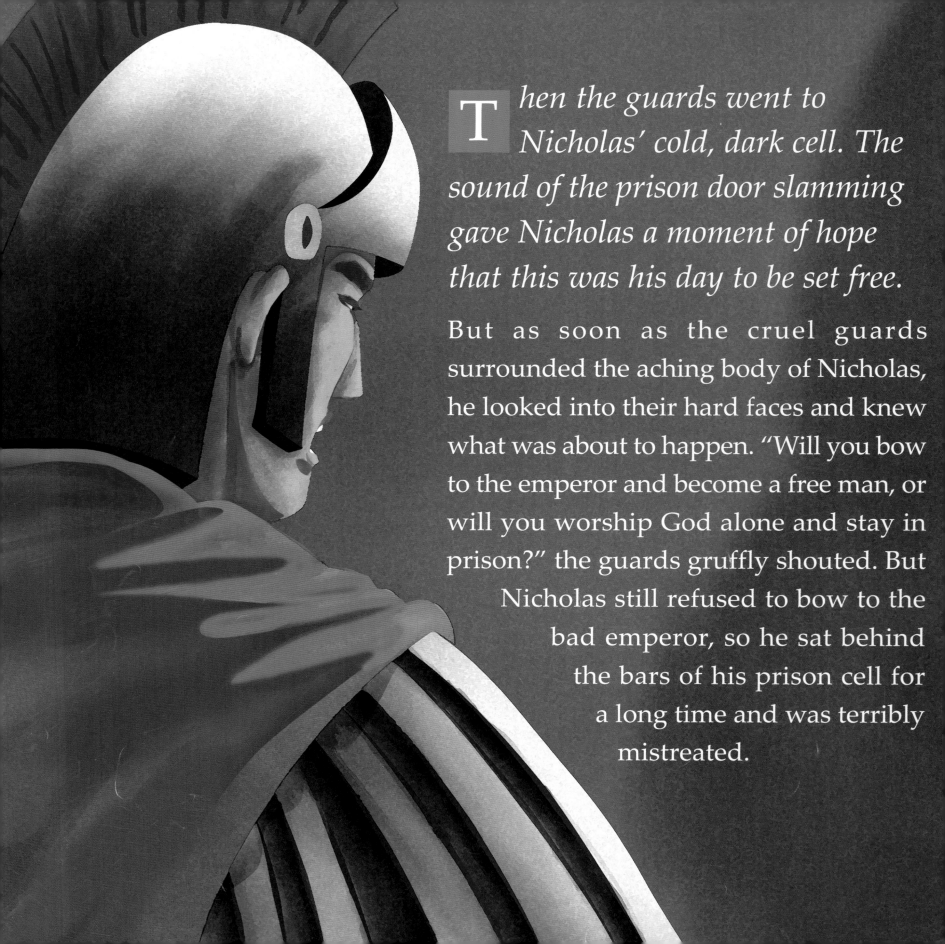

T hen the guards went to Nicholas' cold, dark cell. The sound of the prison door slamming gave Nicholas a moment of hope that this was his day to be set free.

But as soon as the cruel guards surrounded the aching body of Nicholas, he looked into their hard faces and knew what was about to happen. "Will you bow to the emperor and become a free man, or will you worship God alone and stay in prison?" the guards gruffly shouted. But Nicholas still refused to bow to the bad emperor, so he sat behind the bars of his prison cell for a long time and was terribly mistreated.

"Release all the Christians from prison!" declared Constantine.

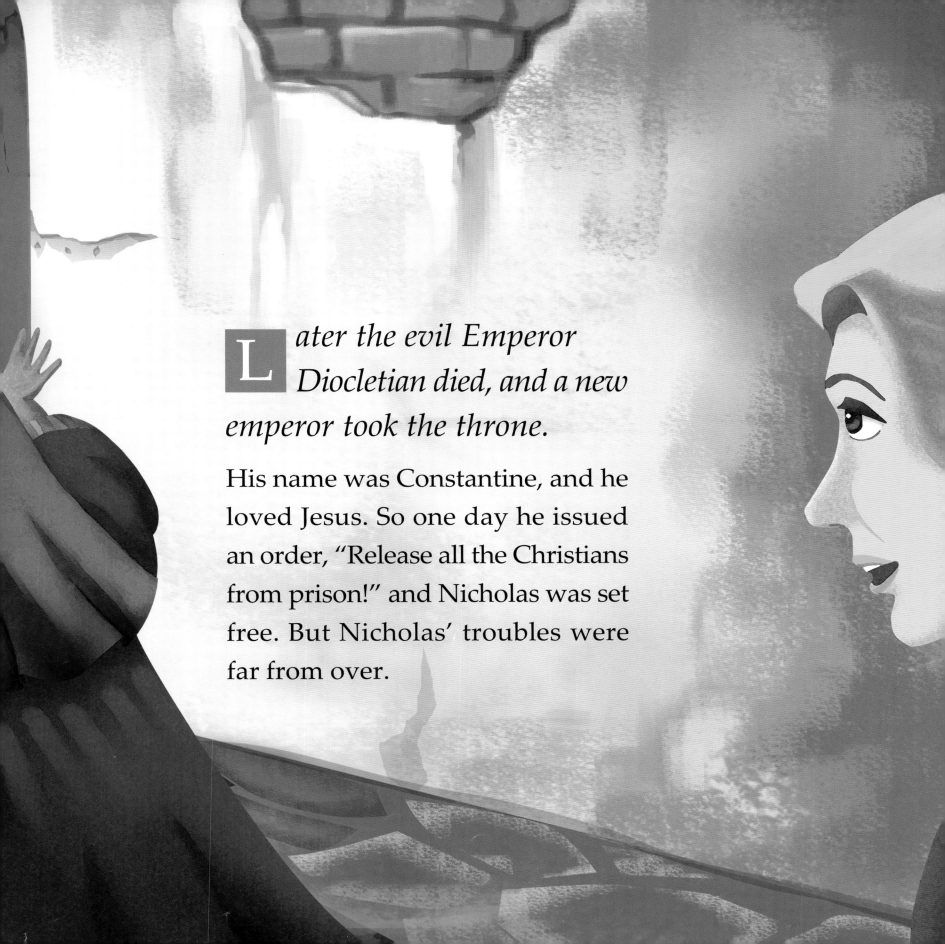

L ater the evil Emperor Diocletian died, and a new emperor took the throne.

His name was Constantine, and he loved Jesus. So one day he issued an order, "Release all the Christians from prison!" and Nicholas was set free. But Nicholas' troubles were far from over.

A leader in the church named Arius began to teach that Jesus was not God who came to earth in the form of a man.

Arius was very wicked and went so far as writing songs that made fun of God. The melodies were so catchy that people would sing them on the streets on their way to school, work and even church. They became very popular.

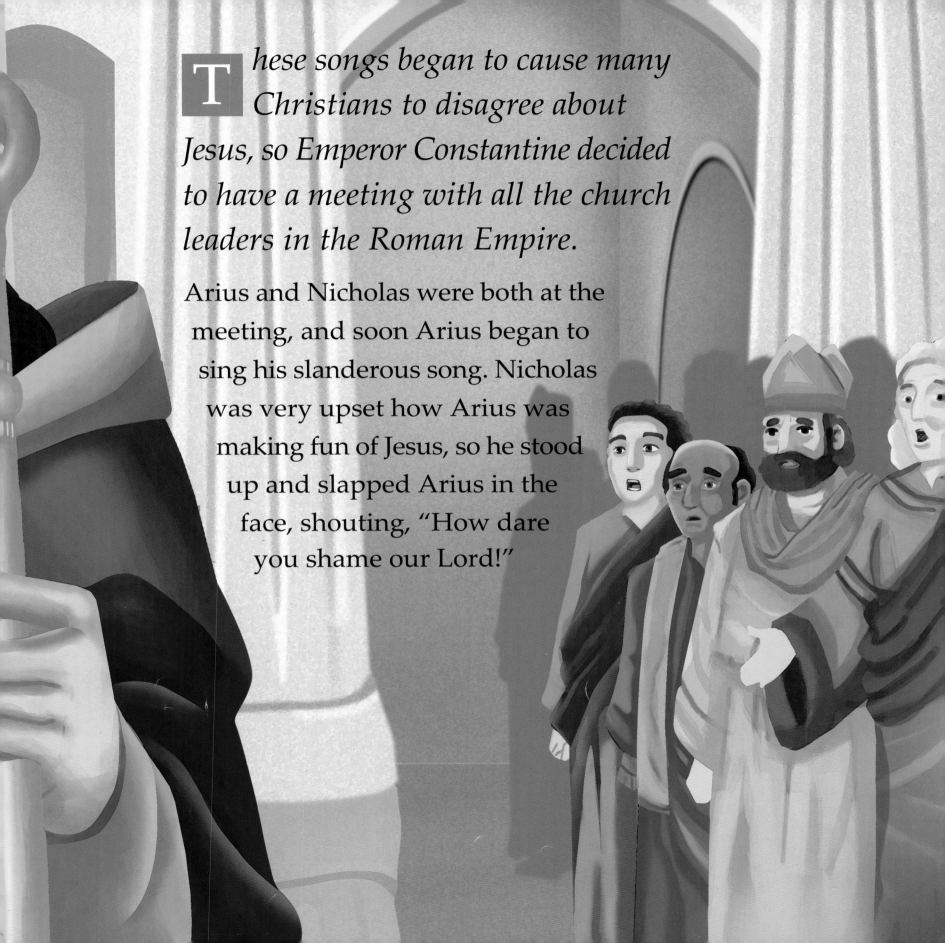

These songs began to cause many Christians to disagree about Jesus, so Emperor Constantine decided to have a meeting with all the church leaders in the Roman Empire.

Arius and Nicholas were both at the meeting, and soon Arius began to sing his slanderous song. Nicholas was very upset how Arius was making fun of Jesus, so he stood up and slapped Arius in the face, shouting, "How dare you shame our Lord!"

T*he church leaders were shocked!*

They knew it was wrong for Arius to sing such a shameful song about their Savior, but they knew Christians were to live a life of peace. So Nicholas was told, "You can no longer preach."

But losing his job as Bishop of Myra did not stop Nicholas from living alongside the poor, caring for the sick and starting orphanages.

He continued to live out his generous heart, until he breathed his last breath.

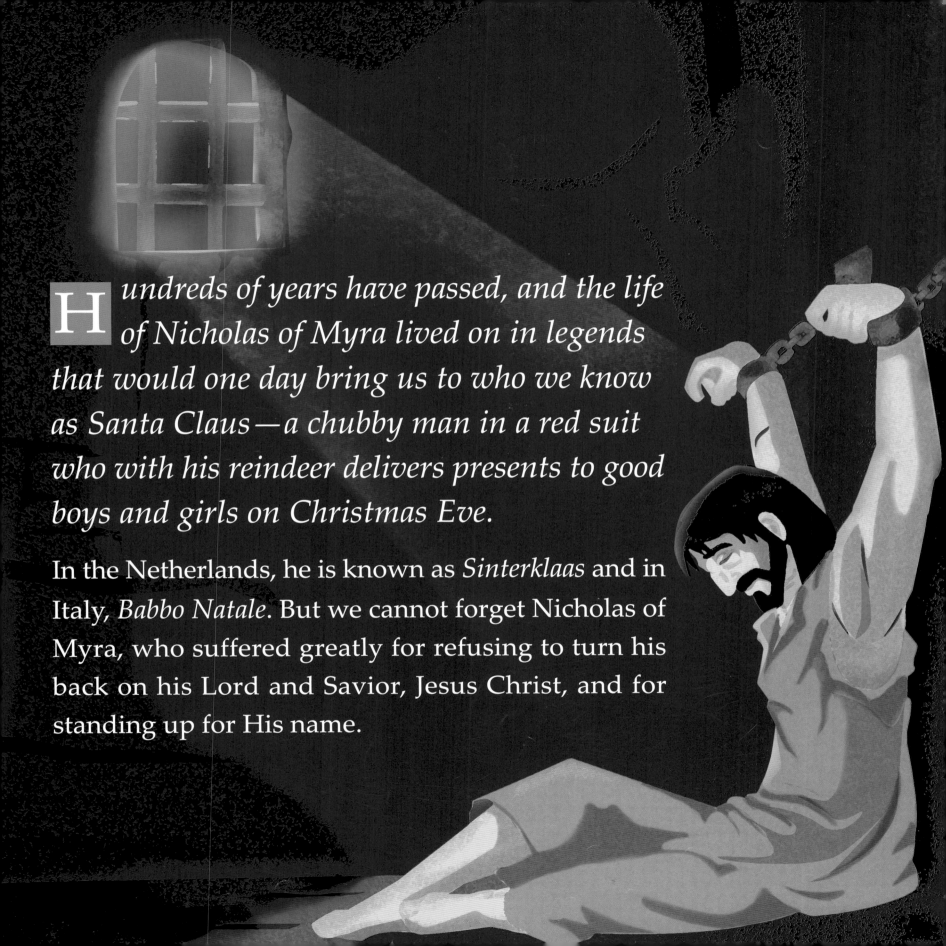

Hundreds of years have passed, and the life of Nicholas of Myra lived on in legends that would one day bring us to who we know as Santa Claus—a chubby man in a red suit who with his reindeer delivers presents to good boys and girls on Christmas Eve.

In the Netherlands, he is known as *Sinterklaas* and in Italy, *Babbo Natale*. But we cannot forget Nicholas of Myra, who suffered greatly for refusing to turn his back on his Lord and Savior, Jesus Christ, and for standing up for His name.

There are nations around the world today where Christians are still put in prison as Nicholas was.

In China, most children are not allowed to learn about Jesus. And in Saudi Arabia, people are imprisoned if caught with a Bible. Their courage to stand for Jesus despite imprisonment and rejection encourage us to live the same way and boldly tell others about Jesus as Nicholas of Myra did.

This Christmas as we celebrate Christ's birth and hear the tales of Santa Claus, may we remember the story of the man from Myra, as well as countless other Christians around the world today who are standing for Christ.

May they encourage us to give generously and live our lives courageously!

For Reflection

"Yes, and all who desire to live godly in Christ Jesus
will suffer persecution."
2 Timothy 3:12

What does it mean to live a godly life?
Why is one persecuted for living a godly life?
In what ways was Nicholas of Myra's life considered godly?
Why was Nicholas persecuted for being godly?
How can your life reflect God's character in your relationships,
job, school and home?

Prayer

Lord, thank You for the cloud of witnesses, like Nicholas of
Myra, who have gone on before us, setting an example of
faithfulness and godliness. Show me ways my life can reflect
Your character, so others may come to know You. Continue
to strengthen and encourage believers who live in nations
that persecute them for bearing Your name.

Amen.